D1505951

TRUMPA THE CHEETAH

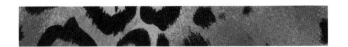

Written by Eduard Zingg

Published by Abdo & Daughters, 6535 Cecilia Circle, Edina, Minnesota 55439

Copyright © 1993 by World Wild Life Films (Pty.) Limited, Postfach 6586, 8023 Zurich, Switzerland

Edited By: Jim Abdo and Bob Italia for Abdo & Daughters Publishing

Text and Photographs: Eduard Zingg
Illustrations and Maps: W. Michel and K. Wozniak

Library of Congress Cataloging-in-Publication Data

Zingg, Eduard, 1940-
    Trumpa, the cheetah / written by Eduard Zingg; edited by Bob Italia.
        p.   cm. -- (An African animal adventure)
    Summary: Introduces animals found in Botswana including the cheetah, duiker, and tsessebe.
    Includes index.
    ISBN 1-56239-214-X
    1. Cheetah -- Botswana -- Juvenile literature.   2. Mammals -- Botswana -- Juvenile literature.   [1. Zoology -- Botswana.   2. Botswana.]
I. Italia, Robert, 1955-   .   II. Title.   III. Series: Zingg, Eduard, 1944-   African animal adventure.
QL737.C23Z58   1993
599.74'428 -- dc20   93-10263
                                                                          CIP
                                                                          AC

Table of Contents

FORWARD

This book describes the wilderness, with its wild animals, and also the original humans of Botswana, the bushmen. Much of what I learned in the Okavango I picked up from Bob. Bob is a native of Botswana and a professional crocodile hunter. I undertook many expeditions with him as I got to know the country and its people better. My camp is more than thirty years old, in the heart of the wild country. My study of the wildlife and the ways of the bushmen forms the basis of this book and the African Animal Adventure series.

From my camp, I've arranged many expeditions over the years. Our purpose was to adapt to the natural world around us. We would visit the gathering places of animals to study and photograph them in their home setting. It is important to know how to approach them; one wrong move will make them run. It is tempting to give wild animals human characteristics. But they will always remain true to their own nature.

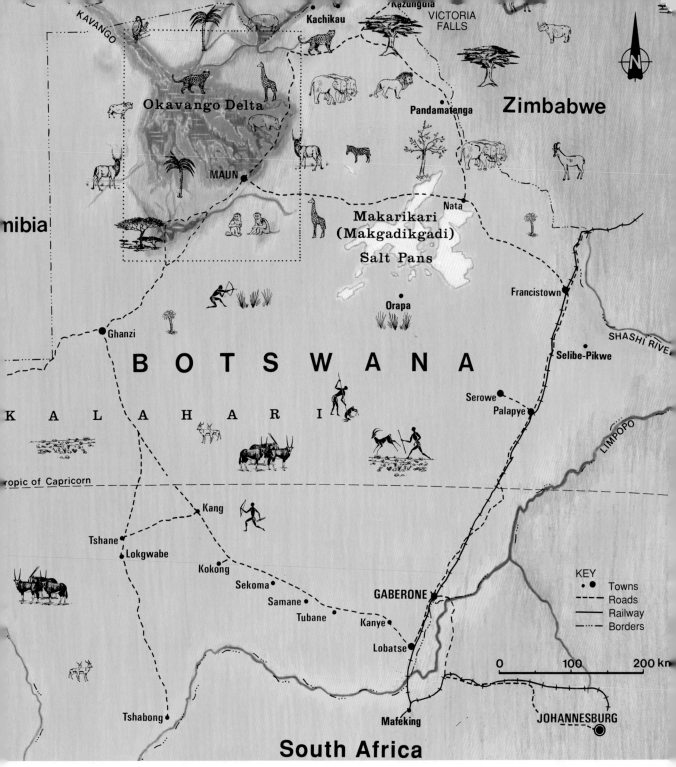

This is a map of the country of Botswana, on the continent of Africa. Botswana is located in Africa's southern region. Many animals inhabit the northern part of Botswana, near the Okavango Delta.

BOTSWANA

My story is set in one of the least-known countries in the world.
I ought to start by setting out some facts about the scene of my
adventures.

The Republic of Botswana (Bots-WAH-nah) is in the southern
region of Africa. It is about the size of France (361,715 sq. miles
or 582,000 sq. kilometers) Despite its size, it is one of the
world's poorest countries. Its population is about 1.1 million
people. The languages spoken there are Tswana (Tis-WA-nah)
and English.

The Kalahari (Kal-a-HAR-ee) Desert is in the heart of Botswana.
It is not the North African type of desert with only sand dunes.
There are scrubs and thornbushes, and it would be possible to
have livestock if only water were available. The terrain is made
up of a complex of rivers and lakes. This area is known as the
Okavango (Ah-ka-VON-go) Delta. Many of the islands are
flooded in the rainy season, during Africa's spring and summer
months. The delta is fed by the Okavango River, which starts in
Angola and ends its course in the Okavango Basin. The
Okavango Delta, with its constant supply of water, is a haven
for all kinds of wildlife.

To enjoy the wealth of wildlife in Africa, a person has to meet
certain physical demands. A person must accept that in the
wild kingdom the animals make the rules; they do not perform
for man's benefit, but merely tolerate his presence. However
human the animals appear to be, the wildlife of Africa are true
to themselves and their own natural habitat.

I know a lot about cheetahs. I ought to. I have reared one like my own child and he lives with me constantly.

CHEETAHS

Cheetahs (CHEE-tahs) have long, slender but muscular legs, making them the fastest animals in Africa. They reach speeds of up to 70 miles/hour (112 kilometers/hour), but not for very long periods of time. Their speed helps them escape from leopards, which are also fast and don't like cheetahs. Cheetahs are often mistaken for leopards, but there are big differences. The cheetah's head is rounder and smaller than a leopard's and its eyes are a yellow-brown color. The cheetah has two black stripes running down its face from the corners of its eyes to the corners of it mouth. The tail is ringed in black. Cheetahs hunt from an ambush. They are shy.

Four to six cubs are usually born. The death rate among cubs is high. They are often taken by hyenas or large birds of prey when the mother cheetah is not around. The cubs are perfect replicas of their mother. They have the two dark lines running like tear stains from the corners of their eyes to the corners of their mouths. The cubs will play unconcerned while the mother hunts for food.

Cheetahs seem to hunt, not by searching for prey, but by remaining in one place until some antelope drifts into the vicinity. When this happens, the cheetah will advance, crouching, slowly moving closer, keeping a watch on its unsuspecting victim.

The slender body and long legs of the cheetah help it to attain speeds of up to 70 miles/hr. (112 km/hr.).

Then it will suddenly start to chase the antelope as it runs for its life. The cheetah will eventually gain on the antelope. The antelope will zig-zag at the last second but the cheetah will follow each turn, then pounce on the antelope.

Cheetahs may be built for speed but like all cats they lack stamina. Their stored energy is expended in one brief burst. Cheetahs will run only as fast as necessary to catch up with and then stay close to their prey until they can trip it. A cheetah hunting alone doesn't prey on anything that weighs more than itself. Cheetahs hunt mainly on the open plains, and prefer to select prey that is fleeing rather than standing around alertly.

Female cheetahs are usually alone except when accompanied by their cubs. The male cheetahs tend to become companions, as the male lions do. Cheetahs possess characteristics of dogs as well as cats. Although they are classified as cats, like dogs they cannot retract their claws. They sit in a dog-like fashion, yet they hunt like the feline family. When eating, cheetahs tear off large chunks of meat without holding their prey. The lion and leopard hold their food to get the best of it.

Because cheetahs are timid creatures, a kill does not mean a meal. Often they give their prey to other stronger animals like the hyena. Cheetahs are very nervous eaters, always glancing around for other animals to attack them. Cheetah cubs run for two years with their mothers who teach them how to hunt. Cheetah cubs have to learn to hunt, because, unlike lions, they cannot depend on a group for food.

*In their home territory, a pair of cheetahs keep a sharp lookout for enemies. The
female will raise the cubs on her own. Lions are the cheetah's most feared enemy.*

One day one of my assistants, Mutero, and I were driving back to camp. We were north of the Okavango Delta. There was thick high grass on both sides of the track. We noticed a bush fire not very far away. It was in the direction of our camp. Bush fires are unpredictable. I checked the wind direction and found that the fire was headed towards the track. We could not continue towards the camp. The air was shimmering with heat, which was becoming intense.

While I was turning the landrover around I saw something moving in the bush on my right. I got out of the truck and found a baby cheetah. I picked it up in my arms. It drew up its paws; the pad of its right front paw was burnt. It had evidently lost its family in the fire. Suddenly I realized the risk I had taken and I pulled out my rifle. The mother might have been nearby. I quickly took the cheetah by the neck and carried it to the landrover. I bandaged its burnt paw and gave it to Mutero to hold. It was now time to move as the heat was increasing. I drove fast to get away from the advancing fire. There was no opportunity to turn left or right. Then I saw a group of antelope crossing the road, indicating there must be a turnoff. In fact there was a way down to the river. All sorts of animals were taking refuge from the blaze. Following some impalas was a monitor lizard which had stopped to get its breath. At the river's edge were all kinds of warthogs and antelope. I turned down towards the river and drove for a couple of hundred yards.

A small herd of elephant came down to the river; they didn't seem pleased to see us. They moved downstream. But the antelopes came closer, all of them thirsty.

I left Mutero in the truck with the cheetah and followed the elephants. They went to a pool to bathe and quench their thirst. One baby elephant was trying to climb the sandy river bank, but kept slipping back down. Its mother finally batted it up with a hefty slap of her trunk.

I went back to Mutero after having a look up and down the riverbank. I was worrying about Joseph (one of my assistants) in the camp, and the camp itself. By this time the smoke was not so dense, indicating that the fire was burning itself out. When the sun set, the fire was more visible. Eventually we moved on to the camp, where Mutero and I were glad to find Joseph unhurt.

Mutero said to Joseph, "I've got a surprise for you." I fetched the baby cheetah out of the truck. He (for it was a he) was a cuddly bundle of long fur, with round ears, two big eyes with eye stripes, and light brown hair. The legs were much longer than those of a leopard or a lion cub. His body was covered with solid spots. He was restless but didn't try to escape. I put him in the tent and at suppertime we tried to feed him. He had no appetite and only drank a little water. For the next two days he was not very active. He tried to bite the bandage off of his paw. He finally began to take an interest in his surroundings. After a while he began to move around the tent and follow me wherever I went, but not near the fire. He preferred the shade to the sunlight, and always laid down behind me, never in front.

Mutero caught a guinea-fowl for the cheetah to eat. For up to two years cheetah parents bring their young guinea-fowl or baby antelope. When Mutero gave the guinea-fowl to the baby cheetah, he took it down to the river, tore it to bits, and ate the whole thing.

Trumpa, the cheetah, as a cub.

VISITORS IN THE WILDERNESS

There was only a week to go before the arrival of Dr. Burns from a zoological institute in the United States. He was coming to take photographs of the animals and the wilderness. The whole group pitched in for the preparations. It was a great pleasure to get back to the bush and to see my cheetah, who I named Trumpa, because he always gets so excited by the sound of elephant trumpeting.

Among our first tasks, we had to set up a landing strip. We also had to set up a tent as a storeroom for groceries. Then we had to build an anthill oven to bake bread. This involves cutting a chimney down from the top of the anthill and making two holes in the sides, one for the fire and one for the bread.

When Dr. Burns arrived, he was pleasantly surprised at the comfort. He had never been to Africa before. Dr. Burns was also amazed at how good the food was. He was pleased at the great animal pictures he took. And he was sad to say good-bye when the airplane came to pick him up after staying for 18 days.

Our next expedition was with two Americans, Peter and Robert. This expedition would extend past the delta and take us in to the Kalahari Desert. Most of our visitors stayed for set periods of time, but it was impossible to have the length of this expedition figured out. This trip involved a bigger responsibility than ever before. But all possible preparations had been made.

My assistant John and his wife stayed behind to look after our camp and the cheetah. It was not easy leaving them for we were not sure when we would be back. I made it clear to John that if we were not back by the time the rains started, he should free the cheetah, and he and his family would have to start walking. His nearest point would be the village of Ngoma (Ng-O-ma), some 120 miles (193 kilometers) from the camp. They would have to walk though dangerous territory filled with lions, leopards and herds of buffalo.

We left the next morning with three landrovers fully loaded. We traveled northwest along the Savuti (Sa-VU-ti) Channel which winds its way through this flat and arid land. For almost a 100 years it lay dry until the 1960s. Waters overflowed the flood plain of the Chobe River. It filled the valley, drawing life to its waters but killing the trees.

THE EXPEDITION

By the evening of the first day we had not even covered 30 miles (48 kilometers). We had been threading our way through a trackless desert area, where the going was tough because of the deep sand.

The second day was even harder. Despite an early start and driving for 12 hours we only covered 10 miles (16 kilometers). The terrain got worse and the travelling was made even harder by the hot sun. Supper was taken in exhausted silence. We slept close to one another, around the landrover, in sleeping bags. The hyenas howled throughout the night, and we heard the first lions at dawn.

*These two landrovers were our only means of travel, and often
our only form of protection from the lions.*

I awoke to the sound of growling. Looking up I saw four lions only about 12 feet away (3.6 meters), staring at us. My rifle was not near me. I threw a handful of sand at Robert's face as he lay sleeping. He sat up immediately. He followed the direction of my pointing finger, and realized what I wanted. He picked up my rifle and slowly brought it to me. Peter was still sleeping and did not know what was going on. Although the lions didn't seem dangerous, they were far too close for comfort. The lions made themselves comfortable, lying down in the grass with their heads sticking out. They watched us the whole time. We stared at each other for more than an hour, playing a game of "who moves first."

I began to doubt whether the rifle was loaded. I decided to check it. I eased the bolt back and it made a noise which scared the lions. The lions disappeared into the bush. Robert and I relaxed and started to discuss the experience. Robert remarked that it was unpleasant to think that we could have been a lion's breakfast. Peter meanwhile slept through everything.

It was nearly midday by the time we left camp, and we made poor progress. As we were enjoying our afternoon tea something made a noise in the grass nearby. I jumped up to see what it was; a duiker eating off of a shrub. As I came closer it turned and fled.

The duiker often goes from one rainy season to the next without drinking any water.

The Duiker

The duiker (DOO-ik-er) is grayish in color with a reddish forehead. It is found all over Africa. A long dark line leads from the base of its forehead to the nostrils. The ears are pointed and long. It has long hair protruding from the top of its head. Only the males have horns out of the forehead. The horns grow straight back in a line with the head. The height is about 26 inches (66 centimeters) and the weight is up to 55 pounds (25 kilograms). Duikers usually live in pairs, but are often seen alone. They prefer well-wooded country. Their diet includes young leaves, seeds and wild fruit.

When alarmed, the duikers first reaction is to crouch in the grass. Then they jump up and follow a zig-zag course, with plunging jumps. This is where they get their African name of *duiker* meaning "diver." When fleeing they often halt to look back. This usually ruins their escape. They sleep during the day and feed in the cool of the evening. Jackals and large eagles prey upon young duiker. The adults are caught by wild dogs, leopards, cheetahs and pythons.

I rejoined the others and told them about how I once saw a wild dog hunt which took place on the other side of the river. Twelve dogs were chasing a female bushbuck. Two of the dogs were running in front of the pack and chasing the buck hard. The rest of the dogs were just trotting along on the sides and to the rear. As the buck tried to swerve to one side, the dogs on that side chased it back.

When the first two dogs got tired they fell back. Two other dogs took their place, so that the buck had to keep running.

After a while the buck began to slow from exhaustion. Seeing this the two lead dogs closed in and began leaping at its sides and belly. Losing a lot of blood, the buck weakened and fell. The dogs closed in on it. They tore it apart limb from limb. Within fifteen minutes it was gone. The dogs growled and snapped at one another. They immediately set out on a new hunt. This time they went after a male bushbuck which fled into the water and swam across. The dogs did not follow and the buck was safe.

There are several types of bushbuck all over the world. The southern African bushbuck is outstanding in appearance and character. It lives in the deep bush. It is rarely seen. It is an excellent swimmer and often takes refuge in the river. Bushbuck are sometimes found in pairs but more often alone.

WILD DOGS OF AFRICA

Wild dogs are built like hyenas but don't have a sloping back. They are about 30 inches (76 centimeters) high, and have very large rounded ears. They are black, white and sandy-yellow in color. No two dogs have the same markings. They weigh between 66 and 88 pounds (30 and 40 kilograms).

Wild dogs are entirely ruthless, and perhaps among the most interesting killers in Africa. They run in packs of six to fifteen. Wild dogs will pick out one victim from a herd of antelope and stick to that creature until they kill it. After a really satisfying meal they will roll and play for a while.

Wild dogs are entirely ruthless, and perhaps the most feared killer in Africa. They are always on the move. After a really satisfying meal they will roll and play around.

I have seen lions and leopards display the greatest respect for wild dogs and move away from areas where they are. Wild dogs prey on duiker, impala, bushbuck and young kudu. They have an unpleasant natural odor. They smell something like old, rotten, uncured animal hides. They are not true dogs, because they only have four toes to each paw instead of five.

No wild animal is hated as much by man as the wild dog. But we must remember that it has its place in nature; it helps to keep the balance by killing sick and decrepit animals.

THE TSESSEBE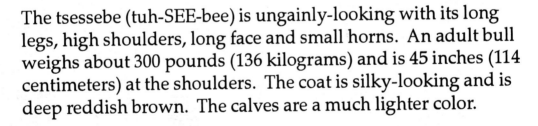

The tsessebe (tuh-SEE-bee) is ungainly-looking with its long legs, high shoulders, long face and small horns. An adult bull weighs about 300 pounds (136 kilograms) and is 45 inches (114 centimeters) at the shoulders. The coat is silky-looking and is deep reddish brown. The calves are a much lighter color.

The tsessebe is the swiftest of the African antelope, with great strength. It can run faster than most race horses. These animals prefer flat country. They roam in groups of about 10.

Tsessebe like shady areas where they shelter during the hot hours of the day. They are extremely curious animals. More than once I have taken refuge under a shade tree and fallen asleep to wake up to a herd of tsessebe standing very close by staring at me.

The tsessebe can survive for as long as three months without water. When the rains return, the tsessebe follow the receding floods, being dependent on fresh grass for food.

On our drive we spotted a group of warthogs at a watering hole. These are very-funny looking creatures resembling pigs.

After three hours we had gone 12 miles (19 kilometers). Suddenly our front wheel went into an antbear hole. We were stuck. "What now?" sighed Peter. I had no answer for him. All day we tried everything to get the landrover out of the hole. The heat made our situation worse. I suggested that we return to camp. We had supper and slept in the landrover.

Peter was terrified and exhausted. He began to imagine figures moving among the trees. He woke me up in the middle of the night saying there was an elephant right next to us. I told him there was nothing there and we went back to sleep. Peter woke me again. To make him happy I got up and walked a few yards into the shadows of the trees. It was very dark with only the light of the moon. Peter was walking behind me. He pointed into the dark and said, "Look there."

By using my imagination I could make out what looked like the shape of an elephant's head. I laughed and asked him if he realized that he had mistaken a branch of a tree for the head of an elephant.

I hoped he would now get some rest. He would need all his strength for tomorrow.

Next morning we had no option but to leave almost everything behind in the truck. We took along a little food and a first aid kit. By dawn we had already covered 2 miles (3.2 kilometers). But as the sun got higher and hotter, the going became more difficult.

While other animals have an air of nobility, warthogs have more homely characteristics. They are peaceful, unobtrusive, and busy animals.

When we were about halfway, we decided to rest. Peter was completely exhausted and stated that he couldn't go any farther. Then he asked me how I knew we were headed in the right direction. I explained that we were walking in the direction of the two hills in front of us. I understood that everyone was exhausted. But we had to keep going if we wanted to get to camp before nightfall. Peter and Mutero agreed with me.

We went on another 2 miles (3.2 kilometers), and then Peter just gave up. He fell to the ground groaning, saying he could not go any farther. We picked him up and laid him under an acacia tree, commonly called umbrella tree. We all rested in the shade. We pleaded with Peter but he was too exhausted to even answer. By this time it was afternoon.

A group of warthogs came down to the watering hole. Two rhinos appeared in the distance, and then a few buffalo. There was an advance group of about 20 to 30, but following them was a herd of several hundred. They kept on pouring out of the bush until we were surrounded by them. This worried me. Where there are buffalo, there generally are lions as well.

This proved to be the case.

A male lion relaxing after a meal. The females do the hunting; the males express their dominance by demanding first place at the food.

In the distance we saw four yellow specks: two lions lying down in the grass and two with big manes standing nearby. Now we had to be even more careful. We had Peter who was sick and the lions waiting to attack.

It was about four o'clock when Peter came to himself again. He repeated that he couldn't go any farther. I told him that he had to, or we would all be eaten by the lions. Peter then forced himself to get up. Leaning on me and Mutero, we began to walk. I could hardly believe that someone so near the end of his rope could get up and walk. Fear of the lions must have done it. This was our salvation.

A beautiful sunset in Botswana.

GLOSSARY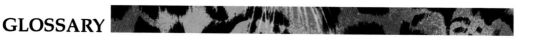

Acacia Tree - a tree from which gum is obtained.

Africa - a continent (large body of land) south of the Mediterranean Sea between the Atlantic and Indian Ocean.

Antbear - a tropical mammal that feeds on ants and termites.

Antelope - a swift-running animal resembling a deer, found especially in Africa.

Anthill - a dirt mound over an ant's nest.

Botswana - a country in southeastern Africa.

Buffalo - a kind of ox found in Asia and southern Africa.

Bushbuck - a type of antelope found in Africa.

Bushmen - members of an aboriginal tribe of southern Africa.

Cheetah - a kind of leopard. Of the cat family, found in Africa.

Chobe River - a river in Botswana, Africa.

Elephant - a very large land animal with a trunk and long curved ivory tusks.

Expedition - a journey for a particular purpose.

Feline - an animal of the cat family.

Guniea-fowl - a bird of the pheasant family, with gray feathers.

Hyena - a flesh-eating animal with a howl that sounds like wild laughter.

Jackal - a wild flesh-eating animal of Africa and Asia, related to the dog.

Kalahari Desert - a dry, arid region of the country of Botswana in southern Africa.

Kudu - a type of antelope found in Africa.

Leopard - a large African and Asian flesh-eating animal of the cat family.

Lion - a large, powerful African and Asian flesh-eating animal of the cat family.

Okavango Delta - an area of the country of Botswana which is plentiful in water and wildlife.

Prey - an animal that is hunted or killed by another for food.

Python - a large snake that crushes its prey.

Savuti Channel - a narrow waterway of the Savuti River in Botswana, Africa.

Tsessebe - a type of antelope found in Africa.

Zoology - the scientific study of animals.

INDEX